SPACE MYSTERIES

WHAT IS ON THE FAR SIDE OF THE MOON?

 Gareth Stevens
PUBLISHING

BY EMILY MAHONEY

Please visit our website, www.garethstevens.com. For a free color catalog of all our high-quality books, call toll free 1-800-542-2595 or fax 1-877-542-2596.

Cataloging-in-Publication Data

Names: Mahoney, Emily.
Title: What is on the far side of the moon? / Emily Mahoney.
Description: New York : Gareth Stevens Publishing, 2019. | Series: Space mysteries | Includes index.
Identifiers: LCCN ISBN 9781538219652 (pbk.) | ISBN 9781538219638 (library bound) | ISBN 9781538219669 (6 pack)
Subjects: LCSH: Moon--Juvenile literature. | Moon--Exploration--Juvenile literature.
Classification: LCC QB582.M34 2019 | DDC 523.3--dc23

First Edition

Published in 2019 by
Gareth Stevens Publishing
111 East 14th Street, Suite 349
New York, NY 10003

Copyright © 2019 Gareth Stevens Publishing

Designer: Katelyn E. Reynolds
Editor: Joan Stoltman

Photo credits: Cover, p. 1 NASA Apollo 16 photograph AS16-3021/Wikipedia.org; cover, pp. 1, 3–32 (background texture) David M. Schrader/Shutterstock.com; pp. 3–32 (fun fact graphic) © iStockphoto.com/spxChrome; p. 5 AlinaXO/Shutterstock.com; p. 7 sdecoret/Shutterstock.com; p. 8 NASA/GSFC/Arizona State University/Wikipedia.org; pp. 9, 21 NASA/GSFC/Arizona State University; p. 10 NASA/Colorado School of Mines/MIT/JPL/GSFC; pp. 11, 15 NASA; p. 13 Encyclopaedia Britannica/UIG Via Getty Images; p. 17 NASA/GSFC/DLR/Arizona State Univ./Lunar Reconnaissance Orbiter; p. 19 NASA/JPL/USGS; p. 21 (close-up) NASA/Wikipedia.org; p. 23 NASA's Goddard Space Flight Center Conceptual Image Lab; p. 25 Castleski/Shutterstock.com; p. 27 NASA/NOAA; p. 29 Romolo Tavani/Shutterstock.com.

Printed in the United States of America

CPSIA compliance information: Batch #CS18GS: For further information contact Gareth Stevens, New York, New York at 1-800-542-2595.

CONTENTS

Words in the glossary appear in **bold** type the first time they are used in the text.

THE MOON

People have always been interested in outer space. It's a beautiful and scary feeling to stare into the night sky and think about what's out there. One of the easiest—and closest!—things we can see from Earth without any special tools is the moon.

How much do you really know about the moon? And what is on the side we can't see? Scientists have studied the moon for years in search of answers, and what they've discovered is amazing!

OUT OF THIS WORLD!

While the moon may look close, don't be fooled. It's actually really far away! The moon is about 238,855 miles (384,400 km) away. How far away is that? That's equal to 30 Earths lined up next to each other!

Earth only has one moon. Mercury and Venus don't have any. Saturn has 62 moons. Jupiter has 69 moons, and scientists have named 53 of them!

THE DARK SIDE OF THE MOON

For thousands of years, people have wondered what's on the back of the moon. They've even nicknamed it the "dark side of the moon." Is it really always dark?

As it turns out, the nickname isn't exactly correct. There's no part of the moon that's always dark. As the moon **rotates**, different parts of its surface receive sunlight. However, it **orbits** Earth at the same speed it rotates, so the same side of the moon is always facing Earth.

OUT OF THIS WORLD!

A better nickname for the side of the moon that we can't see from Earth is the "far side." The part we can see from Earth can be called the "near side."

We can actually see 59 percent of the moon from Earth!
The other 41 percent can only be seen from space.

CRATERS, CRATERS, AND MORE CRATERS

Thanks to space **exploration** and **technology**, we have a pretty good idea of what the far side of the moon looks like. Scientists have discovered that it's actually quite different from the side of the moon we can see.

The far side of the moon has many craters of all sizes, and the ground is bumpy and uneven. It also doesn't have nearly as many of the dark spots, called maria, that can be seen on the near side.

near side of the moon

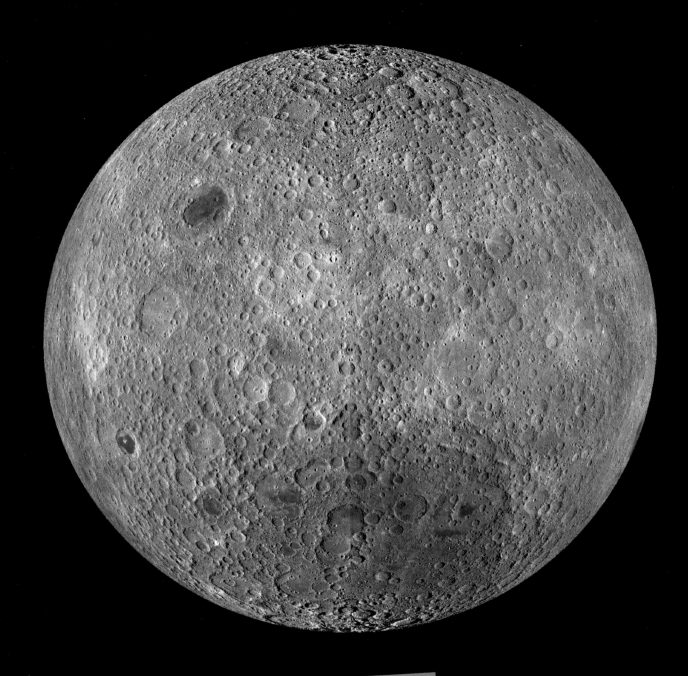

The craters on the far side of the moon are usually wider than they are deep. Some are over 100 miles (161 km) wide!

9

WHY CRATERS?

Billions of years ago, **volcanoes** poured hot, melted rock, or lava, over the surface of the moon. Scientists have found that the crust, or outer covering, of the near side of the moon is much thinner than that of the far side.

A thinner crust on the near side meant more volcanoes and therefore more lava to fill in the craters. The far side of the moon had fewer volcanoes, so its craters are less filled in.

This shows what cracks in the moon's crust might have looked like when its volcanoes were active.

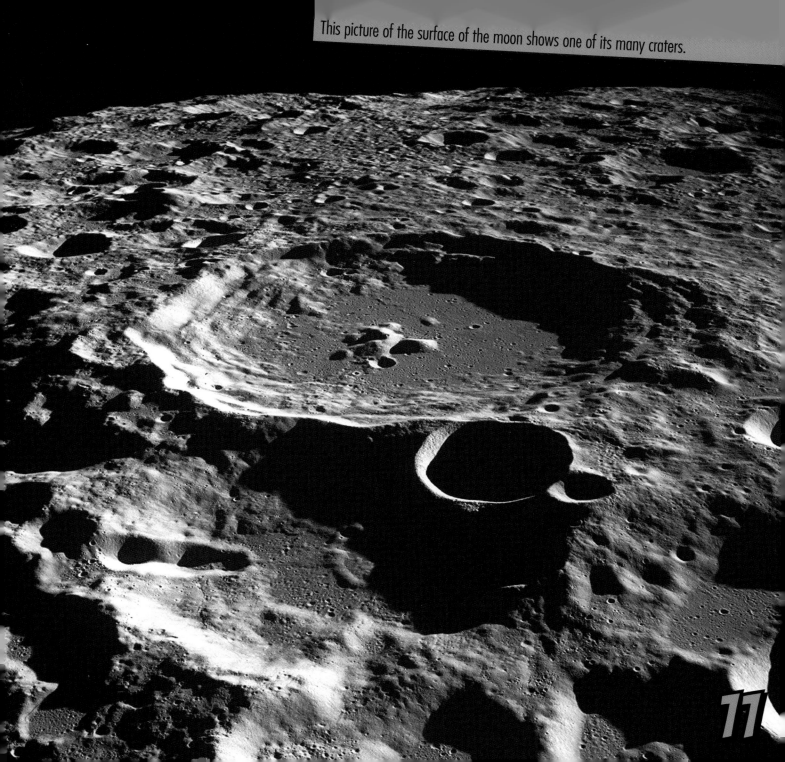

11

FIRST PICTURES

The first pictures to show us the far side of the moon were taken by a spacecraft called *Luna 3*. It was sent up by the Soviet Union (now Russia) on October 4, 1959.

Luna 3's camera took 29 pictures over a 40-minute period of the moon's far side. The pictures showed mountain ranges and two seas that were very different from those on the side of the moon facing Earth. The world was shocked!

OUT OF THIS WORLD!

At first, *Luna 3* had trouble **transmitting** pictures. But by October 18, the spacecraft was able to send 17 pictures back to Earth!

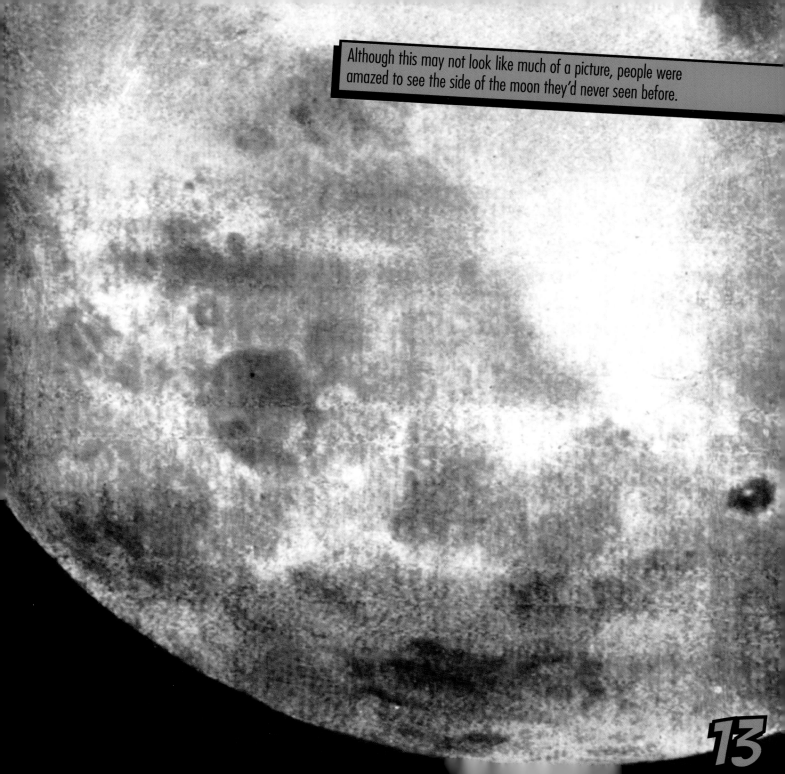

Although this may not look like much of a picture, people were amazed to see the side of the moon they'd never seen before.

13

BETTER PICTURES

Once *Luna 3*'s pictures were out, many scientists were eager to land on the moon. When the *Apollo 11* mission landed the first people on the moon on July 20, 1969, they were only able to explore the near side of the moon. They didn't have the technology yet for exploration on the far side.

But they did have the technology to orbit the moon! So *Apollo 11* took better, more **high-resolution** pictures of the far side than *Luna 3* had.

It took about 4 days for the people aboard
Apollo 11 to make it to the moon from Earth!

15

A HUGE CRATER

While studying pictures of the bottom of the far side, scientists discovered one of the largest impact craters in our solar system. Impact craters form when one object hits another. The South Pole-Aitken basin is a crater 1,615 miles (2,600 km) wide and 9.3 miles (15 km) deep in places!

Scientists aren't sure what hit the moon to cause such a large impact crater to form, but they guess the crater is about 3.9 billion years old!

OUT OF THIS WORLD!

Some scientists think there may be ice in craters like the South Pole-Aitken basin—if there's any water on the moon at all!

The dark purple areas show that the South Pole-Aitken basin is much deeper than other craters on the moon.

17

DID YOU SAY SEA?

A big difference between the far side and the near side is that the near side has many dark areas called maria. The word "maria" means "seas" in Latin. A "mare" is just one sea. However, these aren't seas like we know on Earth, with water, creatures, and sandy beaches.

Back when scientists named these dark spots in the 1600s, it was believed these areas were water. Years later, advances in technology have proven otherwise. Maria are actually flat, sunken areas where lava once flowed!

OUT OF THIS WORLD!

What people once called the "man in the moon" is really just a group of maria that kind of look like the shape of a man's face!

Maria can be seen from Earth without using any special technology.

MARIA ON THE DARK SIDE

While maria are more common on the side of the moon that we can see, there are two very large maria on the far side: Mare Moscovrae, or the Sea of Moscow, and Mare Desiderii, or the Sea of Dreams.

The Sea of Moscow is about 170 miles (275 km) wide. The Sea of Dreams was found to be a small crater later named Mare Ingenii, or Sea of Ingenuity, and several other dark craters.

OUT OF THIS WORLD!

Did you know you can buy land on the moon? One acre (0.4 ha) of land costs about $35, but you'd need a lot of money to buy all the technology and supplies needed to actually live there!

The maria on the moon were formed by volcanoes erupting billions of years ago. When the lava cooled, it was a darker color than the surface of the moon.

Mare Moscovrae

21

THE LRO PROBE

Probes are tools that can travel into space without people inside to drive them. In 2009, **NASA** launched a probe to get better pictures of the far side. It was called the Lunar Reconnaissance Orbiter (LRO). "Lunar" means having to do with the moon. "Reconnaissance" is the study of a region to gain knowledge.

The LRO transmitted much clearer pictures of the moon than those taken by *Luna 3* in 1959. It also showed scientists that the far side has different moon phases than the near side—a shocking discovery!

The 2009 pictures gave scientists a much clearer view of the moon. Thanks to the LRO and other probes, we now have pictures of every part of the moon!

23

IN EARTH'S SHADOW

People have known about moon phases for hundreds of years. The darkness we can see on the moon changes as the moon orbits around Earth. At times, Earth is between the moon and sun, so all sunlight is blocked from reaching the moon. This is called the new moon phase. The moon is "waning" as it heads into a new moon.

When Earth leaves no shadow on the moon, it's in the full moon phase. The moon is "waxing" as it heads into a full moon.

MOON PHASES

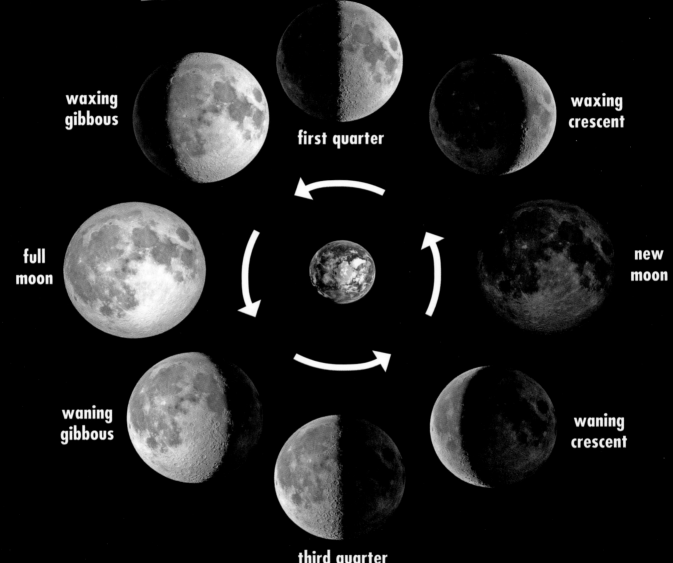

waxing gibbous

first quarter

waxing crescent

full moon

new moon

waning gibbous

third quarter

waning crescent

It takes about 29.5 days for the moon to move through all its phases.

DSCOVR THE FAR SIDE

The Deep Space Climate **Observatory** (DSCOVR) is used to study Earth's climate, or its average weather conditions over time. DSCOVR gathers **information** and pictures from its special point of view in outer space.

DSCOVR also regularly transmits updated pictures and videos of the far side of the moon to Earth! When the moon crosses between Earth and the observatory, DSCOVR has a perfect view of the far side. This gives scientists many new pictures to study!

27

EXPLORING THE UNKNOWN

We've discovered so much about the far side of the moon in the past 50 years, but there's still more to learn! Scientists may one day be able to regularly walk around the moon, collecting bits of the crust and rocks to study and taking closeup pictures of everything.

One day, scientists may even set up observation camps on the moon! Maybe you'll be one of the scientists who studies the moon and makes new discoveries about outer space!

MOON MILESTONES

The moon is about 4.5 billion years old, with many secrets yet to be discovered!

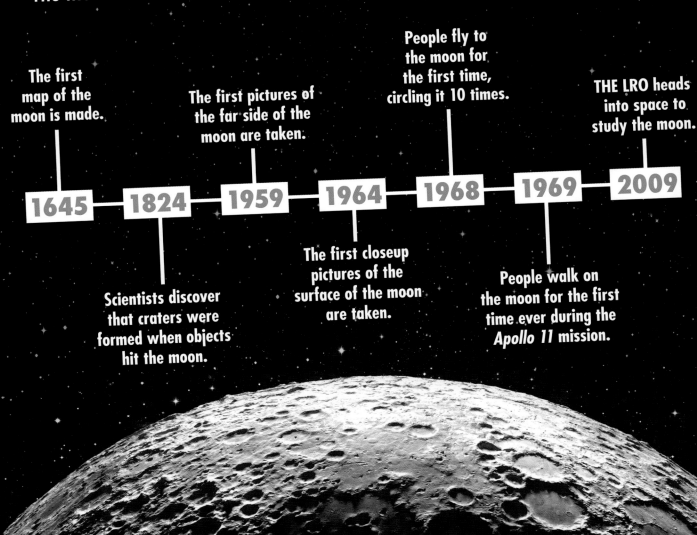

The first map of the moon is made.

The first pictures of the far side of the moon are taken.

People fly to the moon for the first time, circling it 10 times.

THE LRO heads into space to study the moon.

1645 — **1824** — **1959** — **1964** — **1968** — **1969** — **2009**

Scientists discover that craters were formed when objects hit the moon.

The first closeup pictures of the surface of the moon are taken.

People walk on the moon for the first time ever during the *Apollo 11* mission.

29

GLOSSARY

exploration: the act of traveling through an unfamiliar place to learn more about it

high-resolution: good quality

information: knowledge obtained from study or observation

NASA: stands for National Aeronautics and Space Administration, the US government group that travels to and studies outer space

observatory: a place used for the scientific observation of heavenly bodies

orbit: to travel in a circle or oval around something, or the path used to make that trip

rotate: to turn around a fixed point

technology: tools, machines, or ways to do things that use the latest discoveries to fix problems or meet needs

transmit: to send special electrical messages called signals from one piece of technology to another

volcano: an opening in a planet's surface through which hot, liquid rock sometimes flows

FOR MORE INFORMATION

BOOKS

Adamson, Thomas K. *Do You Really Want to Visit the Moon?* Mankato, MN: Amicus, 2014.

Bredeson, Carmen. *Exploring the Moon*. New York, NY: Enslow Publishing, 2016.

Graham, Ian. *Our Moon*. Mankato, MN: Smart Apple Media, 2015.

WEBSITES

All About the Moon
www.scholastic.com/teachers/articles/teaching-content/all-about-moon/
Kids' questions about the moon are answered by a scientist who studies outer space.

The Moon
www.planetsforkids.org/moon-moon.html
This page is filled with facts and pictures about the moon and other objects in space!

NASA Kids' Club
www.nasa.gov/kidsclub/index.html
Games, pictures, and more that can help you learn about NASA.

INDEX